DAYS GONE

REMASTERED

GAME GUIDE

Table of Contents

While Deacon St. John is a lone wolf by nature, the post-apocalyptic world of *Days Gone* introduces several key allies who play crucial roles in his journey. From his closest companions to complex characters with personal stakes in the survival of humanity, these allies help shape Deacon's path and often force him to confront his own values, motivations, and relationships.

Chapter 1: Introduction to the Remastered World

1.1 Overview of Days Gone Remastered

Days Gone Remastered brings the gripping post-apocalyptic adventure back to life with enhanced visuals, refined mechanics, and a smoother overall gameplay experience. Built on the foundation of the original 2019 release by Bend Studio, the remastered edition is tailored for next-gen consoles and PC, delivering improved textures, faster load times, dynamic 4K resolution, and 60 FPS performance.

Players once again step into the boots of Deacon St. John, a former outlaw turned drifter and bounty hunter, navigating the harsh realities of a world overrun by a deadly virus and overrun by infected creatures known as Freakers. Set in the rugged wilderness of the Pacific Northwest, the game combines survival elements, emotional storytelling, and open-world exploration in a beautifully dangerous environment.

In this edition, many of the original's rough edges have been smoothed out—whether it's improved AI behavior, reduced bugs, or streamlined menus. With all previously released DLC included, plus possible new content and quality-of-life improvements, *Days Gone Remastered* offers both newcomers and returning players the definitive way to experience Deacon's journey.

1.2 Key Differences from the Original Version

The *Days Gone Remastered* version is an enhanced iteration of the original 2019 release, offering substantial improvements across visuals, gameplay, content, and overall performance.

These changes ensure that both returning players and newcomers can experience the world of Deacon St. John in a more polished and engaging way. Below are the key differences:

1. Visual Enhancements

The remastered edition takes full advantage of modern hardware, delivering a more immersive experience:

- Higher-Resolution Textures: The game world looks significantly sharper, with more detailed textures for characters, environments, and objects.
- Improved Lighting and Weather Effects: Dynamic lighting and weather systems are more realistic, creating a more atmospheric world. Rain, fog, and the transition between day and night are enhanced to create a deeper sense of immersion.
- 4K and 60 FPS Support: For consoles and PC, the remaster supports up to 4K resolution, delivering crystal-clear visuals. Frame rates are improved, offering a smoother 60 FPS experience, even during intense action sequences.

2. Performance Boosts

The remaster runs significantly smoother compared to the original, thanks to optimizations for modern hardware:

- Faster Load Times: Thanks to SSD optimization on PlayStation 5 and PC, load times are dramatically reduced, whether transitioning between areas, fast traveling, or loading into missions.

- Stable Frame Rates: Where the original had issues with frame rate drops, particularly during combat and large horde encounters, the remaster delivers a stable 60 FPS for a smoother gameplay experience.

---

3. Enhanced Gameplay Mechanics

Several gameplay tweaks have been implemented to improve immersion and playability:

- Improved AI: Both human and Freaker enemies now exhibit smarter and more unpredictable behavior. Human enemies will flank and take cover more intelligently, while Freakers respond with greater urgency, making combat feel more dynamic.
- Better Vehicle Handling: The motorcycle handling has been fine-tuned, with more responsive controls, especially on rugged terrain, making bike exploration smoother and more enjoyable.
- Refined Combat: Melee combat, gunplay, and stealth mechanics have been polished. Stealth kills are smoother, and melee attacks are more satisfying, with better animations and hit detection.

---

4. Content Integration and Additions

The remastered version bundles all additional content and introduces some exciting new features:

- All DLC Included: The remaster includes all downloadable content released post-launch, such as the *Survival Mode*, *Challenge Packs*, additional bike skins, and new weapons, making it the most complete version of the game.
- Expanded Game Plus Features: For players returning for New Game+, additional features or more difficult challenges are implemented, offering a fresh layer of replayability.
- New Easter Eggs and Secrets: Rumors suggest the remastered edition may include hidden collectibles, references, or even new side missions that weren't in the original, encouraging exploration and discovery.

---

5. UI and Accessibility Improvements

The remastered edition introduces significant improvements to the user interface, making it easier to navigate and more intuitive:

- Streamlined HUD: The Heads-Up Display has been redesigned for a cleaner, less cluttered interface. It now offers better information flow without overwhelming the player, such as clearer weapon info, mission tracking, and environmental cues.
- More Customization Options: Improved options for customizing controls, visual settings, and difficulty levels. The remaster also offers more accessibility settings for players with visual or mobility impairments, ensuring a more inclusive experience for everyone.

1.3 What to Expect as a New or Returning Player

Whether you're diving into *Days Gone Remastered* for the first time or returning to the world of Deacon St. John, the experience is tailored to offer something for both newcomers and veterans. Here's what you can expect based on your experience level:

For New Players:

- Engaging Storytelling: The story follows Deacon St. John, a skilled biker and bounty hunter, navigating the dangers of a post-apocalyptic world filled with Freakers (infected humans), hostile factions, and personal loss. You'll be immersed in a gripping narrative that combines emotional depth with intense survival action.
- Open-World Exploration: As a new player, you'll have the opportunity to explore the vast open world of Oregon, filled with dynamic weather, hidden locations, and unpredictable events. The world is open for you to roam, complete missions, and encounter a variety of dangerous challenges, from Freaker hordes to hostile human factions.
- Beginner-Friendly Difficulty: The remastered version includes multiple difficulty settings, allowing you to customize your experience. The "Story Mode" offers a more forgiving difficulty, giving you room to enjoy the narrative without feeling overwhelmed. You can always increase the difficulty as you become more comfortable with the game.

- Learning the Basics: Early on, you'll be introduced to the core mechanics of combat, bike maintenance, and crafting. The game offers tutorial missions that help ease new players into the game's complex systems without being too overwhelming.
- A Sense of Survival: You'll quickly realize that survival is key in this world. Gathering resources, crafting weapons, and managing your bike are all essential for staying alive. The remaster improves the survival systems, making it easier for new players to learn the ropes.

For Returning Players:

- Enhanced Visuals and Performance: Returning players will immediately notice the difference in visual quality. The remastered version supports 4K resolution and 60 FPS, offering a smoother and more immersive experience. The enhanced textures, lighting, and weather effects breathe new life into the world of *Days Gone*.
- Familiarity with Core Systems: As a returning player, you'll be comfortable with the game's mechanics, such as combat, stealth, crafting, and bike upgrades. However, the refined AI, improved combat animations, and vehicle handling make revisiting the world feel fresh and exciting.
- Revised Gameplay and AI: The remastered edition introduces smarter AI, more challenging Freaker behavior, and improved enemy tactics. The larger Freaker hordes are more reactive, and human enemies use better cover strategies, making combat more unpredictable and engaging.
- Expanded Content: If you've already completed the original game, you'll find that all downloadable content

(DLC), such as new challenges, bike skins, and additional quests, is now included. Plus, there may be hidden secrets or minor additions, encouraging exploration and replayability.

- New Game+ Features: For those starting a second playthrough, the remaster's *New Game+* mode offers a chance to carry over your progress with added challenges. The difficulty is increased, and more difficult enemies await, but the rewards are greater.
- Bug Fixes and Polished Systems: *Days Gone Remastered* comes with numerous quality-of-life improvements, bug fixes, and refined systems that address feedback from the original version. Expect a smoother, more seamless experience without the technical issues that might have plagued the first release.

For Everyone:

- Emotional Storytelling: Whether you're new to Deacon's story or already know his journey, the emotional beats and personal stakes remain as compelling as ever. The remaster doesn't alter the original narrative but enhances the experience with better pacing, fewer interruptions, and smoother transitions.
- Replayability: With all the additional content and refined mechanics, both new and returning players will find plenty of replay value. Completing side quests, finding hidden collectibles, and taking on hordes of Freakers will keep you coming back for more.
- More Immersive World: The open-world environment feels more alive and responsive. Freakers behave more dynamically, environments are more interactive, and

every journey through the wilderness can lead to new and unpredictable encounters.

1.4 Tips Before You Begin Your Journey

Before you rev up your bike and set off into the unforgiving world of *Days Gone Remastered*, here are some essential tips that will help you make the most of your journey. Whether you're new to the game or a returning player, these strategies will help you survive the dangers of post-apocalyptic Oregon and enhance your experience from the very start.

1. Understand the Importance of Resource Management

- Fuel is Crucial: Your bike is your lifeline in *Days Gone*, and keeping it fueled is essential. Always try to have extra gas on hand when you set off on a mission, and search for gas stations during your travels. Running out of fuel in the middle of nowhere can be a nightmare.
- Crafting Materials: Early in the game, gather as much scrap, wood, and other crafting materials as you can. You'll need them to craft health items, Molotovs, and, most importantly, upgrades for your bike and weapons. Don't pass up on opportunities to scavenge.
- Manage Ammo Wisely: Ammo is a limited resource, and you'll need to be selective with your shots. Conserve your ammo by opting for stealth whenever possible and using melee attacks when appropriate. Always keep an eye out for additional supplies in camps and hidden areas.

2. Master Stealth and Combat Early On

- **Stealth Is Your Friend:** Freakers can be overwhelming in large numbers, so using stealth can help you avoid unnecessary confrontations. Move quietly, crouch walk, and use distractions (like throwing rocks) to lure enemies away. It's often better to avoid a fight than to engage.
- **Melee Combat:** While firearms are essential, your melee weapon is equally important, especially early on when you might be low on ammo. Learn to use it effectively. Craft and upgrade your melee weapons to deal more damage and handle crowds of Freakers more efficiently.
- **Use the Environment:** Many environments in the game offer strategic advantages during combat. Use cars for cover, climb up to higher ground to take out enemies from a distance, or hide in foliage to avoid detection. Always be aware of your surroundings.

---

3. Upgrade Your Bike Early

- **Focus on Fuel and Storage Upgrades:** Your bike will be your main mode of transportation throughout the game, so prioritize upgrading it. First, work on increasing its fuel capacity and adding storage for additional supplies. A longer-range bike will help you avoid getting stranded.
- **Engine and Performance Upgrades:** As you progress, consider upgrading your bike's engine and handling to make long-distance travel faster and more efficient. A quicker bike is especially useful when you're trying to outrun a Horde or get away from a dangerous situation.
- **Always Repair Your Bike:** Don't neglect your bike's health. Just like your character, it needs regular repairs. Keep an

eye on the condition of your bike and make repairs at any opportunity to avoid breakdowns in critical moments.

---

4. Explore and Complete Side Quests

- Explore the Open World: *Days Gone* features a large, open world filled with secrets, hidden resources, and optional challenges. Take time to explore off the beaten path to find extra supplies, hidden camps, and collectible items that will help you later in the game.
- Side Quests Are Rewarding: While the main story is gripping, side quests offer valuable rewards, including new gear, weapon upgrades, and better relationships with different camps. Completing these tasks not only helps you level up but also gives you deeper insights into the world and characters of *Days Gone*.
- Clear Out Infestation Zones: Infestation zones are areas filled with Freakers. Clearing them will reduce Freaker activity in the area and help you unlock new fast-travel points. These areas are also great for gathering resources, so don't shy away from them once you get the hang of combat.

---

5. Be Prepared for Horde Encounters

- Understand Horde Behavior: Freaker Hordes are massive groups of infected that can overwhelm you in an instant. Understanding how they move, where they gather, and how they behave is key to surviving these encounters.

Use the environment to your advantage by luring them into traps or setting up barricades.

- Upgrade Your Weapons: When facing hordes, your regular weapons may not be enough. Work on upgrading powerful guns, such as the Machine Gun, Shotgun, and Crossbow. These weapons can take down large groups of enemies and help you survive the more intense parts of the game.
- Plan Your Escape: Sometimes, fighting a horde head-on is not the best option. If you're overwhelmed, make sure to know your escape routes. Keep your bike nearby and use it to outrun or avoid the horde if necessary. Always have an escape plan when venturing into Horde territory.

---

6. Settle Into the Camp System

- Factions and Trust: Throughout the game, you'll interact with various camps and factions that are critical to your progress. Each camp offers different upgrades and missions, and building trust with them unlocks better weapons and gear. Focus on gaining trust early to gain access to valuable resources.
- Complete Camp Missions: Camp missions help you earn trust and reputation with different factions. These can range from bounty hunting tasks to helping out camp members. Completing these missions not only rewards you with better equipment but also provides deeper insight into the game's lore.
- Manage Your Reputation: Some camps will offer better rewards and opportunities for upgrades based on how much trust you've earned. Invest time in making sure you're well-regarded in each area to access top-tier gear.

7. Save Often and Use Checkpoints

- Save at Every Opportunity: The world of *Days Gone* can be brutal, and death can come unexpectedly, especially when fighting large groups of Freakers or exploring dangerous areas. Save your progress whenever you can, and make sure to utilize the checkpoints around the map.
- Checkpoint Locations: Pay attention to safe zones and camp locations, as these often serve as checkpoints for your progress. You'll want to use them to restock and save before venturing into dangerous territory.

Chapter 2: Characters & Factions

2.1 Deacon St. John: The Drifter's Journey

Deacon St. John, the game's protagonist, is a complex and emotionally driven character. His motivations and actions are deeply tied to the tragic events of his past, and his personal journey of survival, guilt, and redemption form the core of *Days Gone*.

Backstory

- Former Outlaw Biker: Deacon was once a member of the Mongrels MC, a notorious outlaw motorcycle club. This background gives him skills in combat, survival, and mechanics, which are critical in the post-apocalyptic world.
- Personal Tragedy: The heart of Deacon's story revolves around the loss of his wife, Sarah, who died during the early stages of the Freaker outbreak. Her death, along with the sense of guilt over their separation before the outbreak, haunts Deacon throughout the game.
- The Drifter's Mentality: Deacon is often referred to as "The Drifter" due to his nomadic lifestyle. He prefers working alone and drifts from place to place, helping where he can while avoiding emotional attachments, a coping mechanism born from his trauma.

Character Development

- Struggling with Loss: Throughout the game, Deacon's internal struggle is evident. He is driven by a desire to find closure about his wife's fate, but his journey is also about healing from his past trauma and coming to terms with his decisions.

- Reluctant Hero: While Deacon initially appears cynical and detached, his interactions with others, especially his close allies, reveal a man deeply concerned about others' well-being. His growth over the course of the game highlights his eventual shift from a loner to a more connected and compassionate individual.

Key Motivations

- Find Sarah: The driving force of Deacon's actions is the search for his wife, Sarah. Even though he believes she's likely dead, his determination to find out the truth fuels his actions.
- Survival and Redemption: Deacon's journey isn't just about physical survival, but emotional survival as well. His interactions with his friends, enemies, and the world around him push him toward redemption—coming to terms with his past and finding a new purpose in life.

2.2 Key Allies and Their Roles

While Deacon St. John is a lone wolf by nature, the post-apocalyptic world of *Days Gone* introduces several key allies who play crucial roles in his journey. From his closest companions to complex characters with personal stakes in the survival of humanity, these allies help shape Deacon's path and often force him to confront his own values, motivations, and relationships.

1. Boozer (William Grey)

- Role: Best friend and fellow survivor.
- Backstory: Boozer and Deacon were once part of the Mongrels MC, sharing a deep bond forged through years of friendship and military service. After the outbreak, Boozer became a key part of Deacon's survival, helping him fight off threats and providing emotional support.
- Personality: Despite his tough exterior, Boozer is a loyal and caring friend. He's known for his rough humor and gruff demeanor, but beneath the surface, he's deeply protective of Deacon. He struggles with his own demons, including alcohol abuse and the scars left by the outbreak.
- Importance to Deacon: Boozer's friendship is a cornerstone of the story. Their relationship represents the bond of brotherhood that persists even in a world ravaged by the Freaker virus. His fate and survival drive much of Deacon's motivation throughout the game, especially as Boozer faces peonal challenges that force Deacon to make difficult decisions.

2. Iron Mike (Michael Wilkerson)

- Role: Leader of the Lost Lake Camp.
- Backstory: Iron Mike is a former soldier who now leads a camp of survivors in Oregon. Known for his calm, collected demeanor, Iron Mike prioritizes the safety of his people and works to build a community in the post-apocalyptic chaos. While not as physically capable as others, his wisdom and leadership make him a valuable ally.
- Personality: Iron Mike is a man of principle, embodying a strong moral code that values human life and community over everything else. He is deeply concerned about the mental and emotional toll the outbreak has on his followers, and he tries to ensure that his camp is a safe haven, even if that means making difficult, sometimes unpopular decisions.
- Importance to Deacon: As a father figure to Deacon, Iron Mike often serves as a voice of reason and advice. He offers Deacon guidance and moral support, challenging him to make better choices and consider the greater good. Their bond is one of mutual respect and, at times, tension as they struggle with different approaches to survival.

3. Tucker (Tucker Grady)

- Role: Leader of the Hot Springs Camp.
- Backstory: Tucker is a pragmatic and tough survivor who runs the Hot Springs Camp, one of the many factions that operate in the wilderness. She is fiercely protective of her people and is willing to do whatever it takes to keep them safe and well-supplied. Tucker's methods, however, are often controversial and morally ambiguous.

- Personality: Tucker is strong-willed, resourceful, and unyielding in her pursuit of safety for her people. She is often seen as cold and calculating, especially when it comes to getting resources, but she values loyalty above all else and trusts those who prove themselves useful.
- Importance to Deacon: Tucker plays a significant role in providing Deacon with jobs and missions throughout the game, and she has a complicated relationship with him. While she often clashes with Deacon over his methods and ethics, she sees him as a valuable ally in the fight for survival. Her willingness to make tough choices often puts her at odds with Deacon's more personal, emotional nature.

4. Sarah Whitaker (Deacon's Wife)

- Role: Deacon's wife (deceased, but integral to the plot).
- Backstory: Sarah Whitaker was a scientist working on a cure for the Freaker infection before the outbreak. Deacon and Sarah were separated before the outbreak, and her tragic presumed death haunts Deacon throughout the game. Her memory is a driving force for Deacon's actions as he searches for answers.
- Personality: Sarah was intelligent, selfless, and compassionate, often focused on helping others. She cared deeply for Deacon and was a grounding influence in his life before the collapse of society. Her death marks a significant emotional turning point for Deacon.
- Importance to Deacon: Sarah's memory is one of the most significant emotional drivers for Deacon throughout *Days Gone*. Her death, or rather the unresolved questions surrounding it, pushes him to keep going, even when hope seems lost. Throughout the game,

he clings to the hope of finding closure regarding her fate, and her presence is felt in nearly every aspect of the story

5. NERO Agents (National Emergency Response Organization)

- Role: A mysterious government faction with an agenda regarding the Freaker outbreak.
- Backstory: NERO is a shadowy government faction that remains active in the world after the outbreak, conducting research and attempting to control the Freaker infection. Their motives are not immediately clear, but they hold vital information that could potentially save humanity.
- Personality: The NERO agents are cold, clinical, and unyielding in their mission. They focus on studying and containing the Freaker outbreak, often taking drastic measures to accomplish their goals. Their presence is unsettling, as their true objectives remain hidden throughout much of the game.
- Importance to Deacon: Deacon encounters NERO agents as he investigates the origins of the Freaker virus and uncovers the true nature of the outbreak. The NERO factions provide valuable clues and resources that help Deacon piece together the larger story. However, their secrecy and willingness to make morally questionable decisions make them a source of tension and distrust for Deacon.

6. Ricky (Ricky Spares)

- Role: A fellow survivor and ally at the Lost Lake Camp.
- Backstory: Ricky is a tough, no-nonsense member of the Lost Lake Camp, originally a member of a different faction before finding refuge at Iron Mike's camp. Ricky is a

skilled mechanic and fighter, often helping Deacon with repairs and offering support during difficult situations.
- Personality: Ricky is strong-willed, capable, and practical. She doesn't sugarcoat anything and often speaks her mind, which can lead to moments of tension between her and Deacon. Despite this, she is loyal and has a deep sense of responsibility for the people she cares about.
- Importance to Deacon: Ricky is a valuable ally to Deacon, offering support and sharing her expertise on mechanics and survival tactics. While her relationship with Deacon is initially based on mutual respect and necessity, it develops into a deeper friendship as the game progresses.

2.3 Hostile Factions: Rippers, Marauders, and More

In the post-apocalyptic world of *Days Gone*, survival isn't just about combating the Freakers; it's also about dealing with human threats that have emerged in the chaos. Hostile factions and dangerous groups roam the wilderness, competing for dwindling resources, territory, and power. These factions often clash with Deacon and his allies, pushing them into intense combat situations. The most prominent of these hostile factions are the Rippers, Marauders, and several others, each with their own terrifying agendas and ruthless tactic

1. The Rippers

- Background: The Rippers are one of the most dangerous and fanatic factions in *Days Gone*. They are a group of survivors who have embraced the Freakers as a new form of evolution, worshiping them as the next stage of human existence. Led by the psychotic and charismatic leader,

Leon, the Rippers have completely abandoned conventional human society, turning their backs on any moral code to pursue their chaotic beliefs. They view death and violence as paths to "transcendence."

- Beliefs and Practices: The Rippers engage in ritualistic and gruesome practices. They frequently mark their bodies with the same symbols that resemble the Freakers' markings, often scarring themselves or even mutilating their faces as a way to "become" more like the Freakers. Their ultimate goal is to align themselves with the infected, believing that death is the final step toward becoming like the Freakers—evolved and free from the constraints of human morality.
- Combat Tactics: The Rippers are known for their brutal and unpredictable combat strategies. They will often attack in packs, relying on raw aggression and unhinged violence. They use makeshift weapons like machetes, knives, and clubs, and their ruthlessness makes them a threat to anyone who crosses their path. The faction's chaotic, unpredictable behavior makes them particularly dangerous when encountering Deacon and his allies.
- Importance to the Player: Throughout the game, the Rippers are among the primary antagonists, often coming into conflict with Deacon as he tries to protect survivors and maintain order in the wilderness. They present both a physical and psychological challenge, with their fanatical beliefs and violent tendencies testing Deacon's resolve.

2. Marauders

- Background: The Marauders are a bandit faction that thrives on chaos and lawlessness. Unlike the Rippers, the Marauders are not a cult, but a group of survivors who have chosen to live by a code of brutality and greed. They roam the wilderness, raiding camps, attacking travelers, and stealing anything they can get their hands on. They tend to form small, disorganized groups but are united by their desire for control over resources and territory.

- Beliefs and Practices: Marauders don't follow a specific ideology like the Rippers. Instead, they are driven by pure self-interest. They take advantage of the lawlessness of the world to prey on weaker survivors, looking to secure supplies, weapons, and vehicles to enhance their chances of survival. The Marauders are opportunists, seeking to gain power through violence, intimidation, and theft.
- Combat Tactics: Marauders are highly opportunistic, attacking when they see a vulnerable target. Their tactics are often guerrilla-like: setting ambushes, using traps, and raiding isolated camps. They tend to use firearms, explosives, and other scavenged weapons to overpower their enemies. While not as fanatical as the Rippers, the Marauders are no less dangerous, using their knowledge of the terrain to spring surprise attacks on anyone who crosses their path.
- Importance to the Player: Marauders frequently come into conflict with Deacon, especially when he's on missions to protect or rescue survivors. They are a constant nuisance and threat, often appearing in the wilderness to raid or attack. Deacon will need to clear out Marauder camps and protect vulnerable survivors from their attacks.

3. The Scorpions

- Background: The Scorpions are another dangerous faction in the world of *Days Gone*. This group is highly militarized and well-organized compared to the Marauders. The Scorpions operate out of fortified locations and are armed with military-grade weapons and equipment, making them one of the most formidable threats in the game. They are primarily mercenaries, willing to sell their services to the highest bidder, though their loyalty is driven more by profit than any moral code.

- Beliefs and Practices: The Scorpions are motivated by survival, but their tactics are far more disciplined and calculated compared to other factions. They frequently engage in raiding parties, taking over territories and wiping out any survivors they encounter. Their militaristic nature means that they operate in a highly structured and efficient manner, using advanced combat techniques and weaponry.
- Combat Tactics: The Scorpions are heavily armed with automatic weapons, explosives, and even armored vehicles. They use tactical formations to engage their targets, often laying traps and using cover fire to flush out enemies. Their use of military tactics makes them one of the hardest factions to deal with, especially if you're caught out in the open or without the proper weaponry.
- Importance to the Player: The Scorpions represent a high-level threat throughout the game. Their superior firepower and military discipline mean that Deacon will need to be especially strategic when engaging them. Players will encounter the Scorpions during certain missions, where they will have to clear out their camps or defeat them in specific story-driven encounters.

4. The Freaker Horde

- Background: While not a human faction, the Freaker Horde is one of the most persistent and lethal threats in *Days Gone*. A Freaker Horde consists of large groups of infected humans, known as Freakers, who behave as a unit and swarm anything that poses a threat to their territory. These horde clusters are scattered throughout the world and represent an overwhelming, biological threat to both human survivors and other factions.

- Beliefs and Practices: Freakers don't possess a collective ideology like the Rippers, but they are driven by an insatiable need for flesh. They act in overwhelming swarms, often appearing unexpectedly and descending on areas like a tide of destruction. Unlike typical zombies, Freakers are fast and agile, making them even more dangerous in large numbers.
- Combat Tactics: Freakers attack in overwhelming waves, chasing down anyone who is unlucky enough to be caught in their path. Unlike other human factions, Freakers are relentless and tireless. If a Horde spots you, the only way to survive is to either outrun them, hide, or engage in combat with specialized weapons like explosive barrels, traps, and Molotov cocktails to whittle down their numbers. Freaker Hordes represent one of the greatest environmental dangers in the game.
- Importance to the Player: Freaker Hordes are not only a key environmental challenge but also integral to the game's side content. Deacon can choose to take on these hordes, which serve as one of the game's most intense and rewarding combat challenges. Clearing out a horde rewards the player with valuable loot and a sense of accomplishment. The dynamic nature of the Freaker Hordes makes them an ongoing threat throughout the game.

2.4 Relationships and Side Characters

In *Days Gone*, relationships are at the heart of the narrative, influencing both the emotional depth of the story and the player's interactions with the world. Beyond the core allies, there are several important side characters that help flesh out Deacon's journey. These characters bring personal stakes, varying philosophies, and emotional arcs that enrich the overall experience of the game. Additionally, the game's world is populated by numerous characters whose interactions with Deacon impact his choices and shape his development throughout the journey.

1. Relationships with Allies and NPCs

As you progress through the game, Deacon forms deep, meaningful relationships with many of the survivors he encounters. These relationships are often complicated by the harsh realities of the post-apocalyptic world, where trust is scarce, and survival is paramount.

Boozer and Deacon: The Brotherhood

- Relationship Dynamics: The bond between Deacon and Boozer is one of the most profound in *Days Gone*. They are more than just friends; they are brothers who rely on each other for survival and emotional support. Their relationship is built on years of shared history, including their time in the military and the Mongrels MC.
- Emotional Conflict: Boozer's struggles with his physical and mental health, especially after suffering serious injuries, create tension and vulnerability within their bond. Deacon's dedication to helping Boozer, even at great personal cost, highlights their deep emotional connection. Boozer's fate becomes one of the key motivations for Deacon's actions throughout the game.

Deacon and Iron Mike: Father Figure vs. Son

- Relationship Dynamics: Iron Mike serves as a mentor and father figure to Deacon, providing guidance and wisdom when needed. Their relationship is one of mutual respect, but it is also filled with tension due to their differing approaches to leadership and survival.
- Moral Dilemmas: As the story unfolds, the philosophical divide between Iron Mike's pacifist ideals and Deacon's more aggressive survival tactics becomes a recurring theme. Iron Mike believes in protecting people and trying to rebuild civilization, while Deacon's experiences have led him to prioritize immediate survival.

Deacon and Sarah: The Lost Love

- Relationship Dynamics: Although Sarah is presumed dead for much of the game, her memory is the driving force behind much of Deacon's motivations. Their love story was tragically cut short by the outbreak, and Deacon's grief over her loss defines his character arc.
- Flashbacks and Emotional Weight: Sarah's letters, memories, and the rare flashbacks throughout the game offer glimpses into their past life together. These moments are instrumental in revealing the emotional depth of Deacon's character and how he deals with the trauma of losing her.

2. Side Characters: The Supporting Cast

In addition to the key allies, *Days Gone* introduces a wide array of side characters who help bring the world to life. While these characters may not have the same level of involvement as the main cast, their stories and missions contribute significantly to the game's richness.

Ricky (Ricky Spares)

- Role: A mechanic and fellow survivor at Lost Lake Camp.
- Importance: Ricky plays a key role in helping Deacon with bike repairs and offers support during various missions. She is pragmatic and competent, but her emotional growth throughout the game is important to the larger narrative. She often becomes a bridge between Deacon and Iron Mike, advocating for practical action in the face of difficult decisions.

Manny (Manuel Quintero)

- Role: A mechanic at the Hot Springs Camp.
- Importance: Manny is one of the more colorful characters in the game, known for his humorous and sometimes sarcastic remarks. While he may not have the same emotional depth as some of the other characters, Manny provides useful dialogue and lightens the tone during intense moments. He is also involved in some of the more minor side quests.

Addy (Addy Walker)

- Role: Medic at the Lost Lake Camp.
- Importance: Addy is a no-nonsense character with a deep sense of duty. As the medic at the camp, she plays a vital role in ensuring the survivors' health and well-being. Her relationship with Deacon is more professional, but she has a caring side that comes through when she offers medical support to Deacon or other characters. She represents the caregivers in this harsh world.

Nikki (Nikki Trowbridge)

- Role: A survivor and member of the Lost Lake Camp.
- Importance: Nikki is a minor character who plays a role in some side missions. Her relationship with the main cast is less prominent, but her backstory and struggles contribute to the sense of community within the camp.

---

3. Relationships with Factions

Throughout the game, Deacon's relationships with various factions also influence the world around him. These factions, some of which are hostile and others that offer valuable resources, play an integral role in how Deacon interacts with his environment.

The Lost Lake Camp

- Relationship with Deacon: This camp is where Deacon finds a sense of community, particularly with Iron Mike and Boozer. The people at Lost Lake are generally survivors who value safety, cooperation, and rebuilding society. Deacon's relationship with them is one of mutual respect, but his outsider nature sometimes causes friction.
- Faction Dynamics: As Deacon becomes more involved in the Lost Lake faction, he is faced with moral dilemmas about the camp's leadership and their approach to survival. His interactions with members like Ricky and Iron Mike deepen his ties to the camp, but also force him to question what it means to build a sustainable society in such a broken world.

The Hot Springs Camp

- Relationship with Deacon: Led by Tucker, the Hot Springs Camp operates with a more ruthless and survivalist mentality. The relationship between Deacon and Tucker is often strained, as she takes a more utilitarian approach to survival, focusing on securing resources and maintaining power.
- Faction Dynamics: Deacon's missions for Hot Springs involve handling some morally ambiguous tasks, such as dealing with enemy survivors or engaging in activities that question the ethics of survival. While he occasionally allies with Hot Springs for practical reasons, their methods put them at odds with Deacon's more personal sense of justice.

The Rippers

- Role: Hostile faction and major antagonists.
- Backstory: The Rippers are a dangerous, cult-like group that thrives on chaos and violence. Led by a charismatic and brutal leader, they view the Freakers as a new evolution of humanity and seek to become like them. The Rippers are a major threat to Deacon and his allies.
- Importance to Deacon: The Rippers are one of Deacon's most significant adversaries in the game. Their twisted beliefs and brutal tactics make them a constant menace to the communities Deacon is trying to protect. Their presence forces Deacon into violent confrontations and moral quandaries as he defends his people.

Marauders

- Role: Hostile faction, enemies of Deacon.
- Backstory: Marauders are ruthless, bandit-like survivors who raid camps, steal resources, and terrorize the weak.

Unlike the more structured Rippers, Marauders are chaotic and opportunistic, using violence as a means of survival.

- Importance to Deacon: Marauders often appear as enemies during missions, raiding camps and attacking survivors. Deacon is forced to eliminate them or protect his allies from their attacks. Their unpredictable nature makes them a constant threat in the wasteland.

---

4. Romance and Personal Connections

Although *Days Gone* is not a traditional romance-focused game, there are moments where relationships between characters—especially Deacon and Sarah—offer a glimpse into the personal connections that keep them going in such a harsh world. Deacon's love for Sarah is a central emotional thread throughout the game, providing him with a reason to survive and seek redemption.

- Deacon and Sarah's Flashbacks: Throughout the game, flashbacks to Deacon and Sarah's life together offer a glimpse of a happier time, showing their deep emotional connection. These memories are bittersweet and serve as an anchor for Deacon as he navigates the trauma of the present.

Chapter 3: World Exploration & Map Guide

3.1 The Regions of Oregon: A Breakdown

In *Days Gone*, the world of Oregon is vast and diverse, offering players a range of environments to explore and survive in. Each region has its unique challenges, geography, wildlife, and factions, making the journey feel dynamic and engaging. As Deacon, you'll travel through different zones, each offering new missions, challenges, and opportunities. The world is interconnected, with some areas becoming accessible only after certain milestones in the story. Here's a breakdown of the major regions in Oregon that you'll encounter in the game.

1. The Cascade Wilderness

- Overview: The Cascade Wilderness is one of the first regions you'll explore in *Days Gone* and sets the tone for the environment players will have to navigate. It features a mix of lush forests, mountainous terrain, and winding roads.
- Key Features:
    - Dense Forests: This area is teeming with wildlife, dangerous Freakers, and hostile factions. The dense trees provide ample cover but also hinder visibility, making combat more tactical.
    - First Encounters with Factions: You'll first encounter Marauders and the Rippers in this area, and it serves as a testing ground for learning how to deal with hostile factions and Freakers.

- o Survival Challenges: The terrain is difficult to navigate, and there are plenty of cliffs and rivers that will challenge Deacon's bike travel.
- Story-Related Events: The region is central to the early part of the story, where Deacon meets key allies like Boozer and begins to get involved with the larger community of survivors. It's also where players get their first major introduction to *Days Gone*'s open-world mechanics.

2. The Lost Lake

- Overview: The Lost Lake region is a crucial area for Deacon's journey. It is home to the Lost Lake Camp, a safe haven for survivors, and plays a significant role in the storyline as you interact with various characters.
- Key Features:
    - o Rolling Hills and Lakes: The landscape is characterized by rolling hills and a serene lake that provides a stark contrast to the chaos of the world outside. The natural beauty here hides the dangers lurking in the form of hostile factions.
    - o Camp Dynamics: The Lost Lake Camp is a central hub for the story, where Deacon interacts with allies like Iron Mike, Boozer, and other survivors. The camp serves as a safe base of operations where you'll accept new missions and upgrade your bike.
    - o Ripper Activity: The Lost Lake region is frequently threatened by Rippers, who view this area as a prime target for their violent ideology.
- Story-Related Events: The Lost Lake is where Deacon's emotional journey intensifies, particularly as he helps Boozer recover from an injury. It's also a location tied to

some of the game's major moral choices, as the faction dynamics of Lost Lake come into play.

3. The Highway 97 Corridor

- Overview: The Highway 97 region is one of the more expansive and dangerous parts of Oregon. It's an open, desolate highway surrounded by mountainous terrain, full of wild animals, Freakers, and hostile factions. It's a key area for those looking for larger combat zones and exploration.
- Key Features:
    - Wide Open Roads: The open highway gives players more freedom to navigate large distances on their bike. However, it's not without risks—this area is a hotspot for ambushes, Freaker attacks, and enemy factions like the Marauders.
    - Dynamic Weather and Day/Night Cycles: The weather changes often in this region, with fog, rain, and thunderstorms affecting visibility and gameplay.
    - Hordes of Freakers: The Highway 97 Corridor is home to multiple Freaker hordes, large groups of infected that present one of the most difficult combat challenges in the game.
- Story-Related Events: The Highway 97 region serves as a major checkpoint for Deacon as he travels to meet other survivors and factions. This area also marks a shift in the game's pacing, where large-scale confrontations become more common, and the stakes grow higher.

4. The Siskiyou Mountains

- Overview: The Siskiyou Mountains are one of the more treacherous and mountainous regions in *Days Gone*. This area's steep inclines and rough terrain offer an additional challenge for traversal.
- Key Features:
  - Difficult Terrain: The mountainous roads and rocky paths make it harder to use your bike and navigate, especially when racing against time or avoiding enemy factions. Steep cliffs, narrow passes, and dense forests will keep you on your toes.
  - Bandit Camps and Freaker Nests: The region is home to several bandit camps, including Marauder hideouts, and dangerous Freaker nests. Players will need to clear these out for progress.
  - Weather: The weather conditions in this area can vary significantly, from heavy rainfall to snowstorms, adding complexity to Deacon's travel.
- Story-Related Events: As a higher-level area, the Siskiyou Mountains are where the stakes truly begin to rise. You'll face tougher enemies and increasingly difficult environmental conditions. This region also serves as the backdrop for some of the game's most emotionally intense moments.

5. The Crater Lake

- Overview: The Crater Lake area is the final region you'll explore in *Days Gone*. It's a stunning location filled with lakes, rivers, and high-altitude forests, but it's also one of the most dangerous.
- Key Features:

- o Breathtaking Views: The scenery in this region is absolutely beautiful, with expansive vistas and deep blue lakes surrounded by rugged cliffs. The area contrasts heavily with the dark and gloomy atmosphere in other regions.
  - o Increased Enemy Presence: The Crater Lake area sees an increased presence of enemy factions, including larger, organized groups and more formidable adversaries.
  - o Freaker Horde Locations: As one of the last areas to be unlocked, Crater Lake is home to some of the largest Freaker hordes, requiring strategy and resourcefulness to defeat.
- Story-Related Events: This is where Deacon's journey reaches its climax, as the remaining major story events and decisions take place here. The stakes are at their highest, and the conclusion of key character arcs is set against the dramatic backdrop of Crater Lake.

3.2 Fast Travel & Checkpoints

Fast travel is a vital mechanic in *Days Gone*, allowing you to cover long distances quickly and efficiently. However, it isn't as simple as just selecting a destination. The game's design encourages players to engage with the world and take their time, but fast travel is a necessary convenience for getting through the vast and often dangerous landscape of Oregon.

1. Fast Travel Locations

Fast travel in *Days Gone* requires players to access specific locations known as Checkpoints. These checkpoints are located throughout the world, and once discovered, Deacon can use them to quickly transport to various points of interest. Checkpoints can be found at:

- Nero Checkpoints: These are remnants of the government's emergency response during the outbreak. They are scattered throughout the world, containing important resources like fuel, crafting materials, and even Nero injectors that boost Deacon's abilities.
- Camps: The various survivor camps (Lost Lake, Hot Springs, etc.) act as major hubs for fast travel, allowing you to quickly navigate between regions that have already been unlocked.
- Safehouses: These are smaller locations scattered throughout the world where you can rest and fast travel. They are often surrounded by danger, so make sure to clear out nearby threats before using them.
- Fuel Requirements: Unlike traditional fast travel systems in other games, fast travel in *Days Gone* requires fuel. Deacon must keep an eye on his fuel reserves, as traveling without enough fuel will force you to either gather more or travel on foot.

2. Fast Travel Restrictions

There are several restrictions when using fast travel in *Days Gone*:

- Enemy Presence: Fast travel is not possible if there are enemies nearby. If you're within a zone populated by Freakers, Marauders, or other hostile factions, you'll need to clear the area before fast traveling.
- Time of Day: Fast travel is only available during the daytime unless you have specific upgrades. If you're

trying to travel during the night, the risk of running into hordes of Freakers or other threats increases.

- Increased Risk at Night: Fast traveling at night opens you up to higher risks, as more dangerous Freaker variants come out during the dark hours. Consider whether it's worth the danger before fast traveling at night.

3. Checkpoints and Safehouses

- Using Safehouses: Safehouses are typically small camps set up by survivors where you can rest, resupply, and fast travel to other locations. These areas are relatively safe and often have a few basic supplies available.
- Unlocking New Checkpoints: As you progress through the game, new checkpoints will become accessible. These locations are marked on your map, and you can unlock them by clearing out enemy presence and securing the area for fast travel use.

4. Considerations for Fast Travel Strategy

- Resource Management: Since fast travel requires fuel, it's important to manage your resources efficiently. If you're running low on fuel, you may find yourself stranded in dangerous areas without a way to fast travel, so make sure to always keep an eye on your fuel reserves.
- Strategic Fast Travel: Use fast travel strategically to minimize risks when navigating across large areas. Sometimes it's better to explore on foot or by bike, but when you're low on time or resources, fast travel can save you precious moments.

3.3 Dynamic Weather & Time of Day Effects

The dynamic weather and time of day in *Days Gone* significantly impact the gameplay experience. The ever-changing environment adds both immersion and complexity to the game, affecting everything from visibility to enemy behavior. Players must adapt their strategies based on the weather and time of day to survive in the harsh world of Oregon.

---

1. Weather Effects on Gameplay

- Rain & Fog: Weather conditions like rain and fog can drastically reduce visibility, making it harder to spot enemies or navigate. This can be particularly challenging when trying to avoid or fight off Freakers, who may be lurking just out of sight. The rain also creates mud and slippery roads, making riding your bike more difficult and dangerous. The rain can also mask the sounds of approaching enemies, making you more vulnerable to ambushes.
    - Combat Impact: The rain can make combat more difficult, as your shots may not travel as far and enemies can move undetected in the reduced visibility. It's also harder to hear footsteps or enemy chatter, which could lead to surprise attacks. However, it can also provide an opportunity for stealth, as enemies may not be able to detect you as easily when you're hidden in fog or rain.
    - Strategic Advantage: Use the weather to your advantage when sneaking through enemy camps or avoiding large groups of Freakers. The rain may

dampen the sound of your footsteps, giving you a better chance to slip past hostile groups unnoticed.

2. Time of Day Effects

- **Day vs. Night:** The time of day plays a major role in *Days Gone*'s gameplay, as certain threats and resources are more prominent at different times. During the day, the world is relatively safer, with fewer Freakers and hostile factions roaming the land. It's the ideal time to explore, gather resources, and complete missions without much risk.
    - **Freaker Behavior:** As the sun sets, the behavior of Freakers changes dramatically. They become more aggressive, and more dangerous variants of Freakers come out at night, including the more powerful Newtsand Runners, who are much quicker and more lethal than their daytime counterparts. Larger Freaker Hordes also tend to be more active at night, making travel riskier.
    - **Resource Gathering:** During the day, you'll find more survivors and merchant camps, where you can trade, gather supplies, or get new quests. However, night tends to be quieter in terms of human encounters, but you'll have to deal with the increased risk from Freakers.
    - **Tactical Play:** If you need to take on a Freaker Horde or explore dangerous areas, consider doing so during the night, as the visibility will be lower, but the dangers will be much greater. Conversely, daytime is safer for exploration but comes with

fewer challenges. Adjust your approach to missions and exploration accordingly.

3. The Impact of Weather on Your Bike

- Handling in Rain: The rain significantly affects your bike's performance. The roads become slippery, and turning sharp corners becomes more challenging. The terrain can be difficult to navigate, and sudden drops or bumps in the road are harder to spot in the rain.
  - Fuel and Maintenance: Weather conditions also affect your bike's fuel consumption and maintenance. Rain might force you to drive more carefully, using more fuel as you slow down to avoid losing control. Muddy roads can also be taxing on the engine, leading to faster bike wear.
  - Bike Upgrades: To counteract the effects of harsh weather, upgrading your bike with better tires, engines, and handling systems can help you maintain control even during the worst weather conditions.

4. Storms and Special Events

- Thunderstorms: Thunderstorms can provide some of the most dramatic moments in *Days Gone*. The flashes of lightning can temporarily illuminate the world around you, making it easier to spot enemies or hidden objects. However, the intense lightning and loud thunder can also give away your position to nearby enemies.
  - Horde Movement: When it's stormy, large Freaker Hordes can become disoriented or move erratically, giving you an advantage if you're looking to take them down. However, navigating

the storm can make it difficult to spot them until they're nearly on top of you.
- o Environmental Hazards: During severe storms, you may encounter other hazards, like downed trees, flooded roads, and blocked paths, which could hinder your progress. Be ready to take a detour or wait for the storm to pass.

3.4 Hidden Locations & Points of Interest

In *Days Gone*, the world of Oregon is full of hidden locations, points of interest, and secrets waiting to be uncovered. These areas often contain valuable resources, hidden lore, or challenging encounters that reward exploration. Many of these locations are off the beaten path and can only be discovered by venturing into the wilderness and searching thoroughly.

1. Nero Checkpoints & Labs

- Nero Checkpoints: Throughout Oregon, you'll find several Nero Checkpoints, which were part of the government's effort to control the outbreak. These locations contain valuable supplies, including Nero injectors, which increase Deacon's health, stamina, and focus. The checkpoints also provide story-related lore, shedding light on the events leading up to the outbreak.
  - o How to Unlock: You'll need to clear out any hostile factions or Freakers in these locations to gain access. Once you've cleared the area, you can enter the checkpoint and search for valuable resources like ammunition, fuel, and crafting materials.

2. Hidden Freaker Nests

- Freaker Nests: Scattered throughout Oregon, there are hidden Freaker Nests, which are infested areas where Freakers spawn and take shelter. These nests often require Deacon to clear them out to make the surrounding area safer. Clearing nests rewards players with valuable items and makes exploration safer.
    - Tactics for Clearing: Destroying Freaker Nests requires fire-based weapons like Molotov cocktails or a flame-thrower. However, destroying a nest will trigger a Freaker swarm, so it's essential to plan your attack carefully and be prepared for the oncoming wave.

3. Hidden Camps & Outposts

- Hidden Survivor Camps: In addition to the major camps like Lost Lake, there are smaller, hidden survivor camps scattered around the world. These locations are typically tucked away in remote areas and offer additional quests, supplies, or lore.
    - Bandit Outposts: Some outposts are controlled by Marauders or other hostile factions. These areas are often filled with valuable loot, but they also present significant danger. Clearing these outposts will give you control over the area, making it safer to travel through.

4. Special Landmarks & Easter Eggs

- Landmarks: Oregon is dotted with special landmarks, such as abandoned amusement parks, destroyed cities, or military bases. These locations often hold hidden lore or rewards, offering players a break from the standard gameplay and encouraging exploration.

- Easter Eggs: As with many open-world games, *Days Gone* contains various Easter eggs for observant players. These might be references to other games, movies, or pop culture, and finding them is a fun bonus for those who enjoy hunting for secrets.

Chapter 4: Missions, Storyline & Progression

4.1 Main Story Missions Explained

In *Days Gone*, the main story missions are the backbone of the game's narrative, guiding Deacon St. John through the brutal and unforgiving world of post-apocalyptic Oregon. These missions provide insight into the game's central story, the relationships between key characters, and Deacon's emotional journey as he faces both external threats and personal demons. Each mission progresses the plot, introduces new characters, and challenges the player with different gameplay mechanics.

1. Prologue: Deacon's Past & The Outbreak

- Mission Overview: The prologue sets the stage for Deacon's journey. It introduces players to his life before the outbreak and shows the events leading up to the collapse of society. The opening moments of the game involve Deacon and his wife, Sarah, attempting to escape the chaos of the world as the virus begins to spread.
  - Key Objectives:
    - Escape from the chaos in the city.
    - Make difficult choices regarding Deacon's wife, Sarah, and their plans for survival.
    - Establish the emotional backdrop for Deacon's motivations, setting up the personal stakes of his journey.
  - Story Impact: This mission is pivotal in setting up Deacon's emotional arc, as the loss of his wife and his inability to save her is a driving force behind his actions throughout the game. It's also the

foundation for his complicated relationship with Boozer, his close friend, and the story's ongoing struggle between hope and despair.

2. "Surviving the Collapse"

- Mission Overview: After the prologue, Deacon begins his journey in the world of Oregon, struggling to survive in the aftermath of the collapse. The first few missions introduce the basics of survival, including scavenging for food, clearing out Freaker nests, and establishing a foothold in the wilderness.
  - Key Objectives:
    - Clear out enemy camps of Marauders and other hostile factions.
    - Gather important supplies like fuel, crafting materials, and ammunition.
    - Start building relationships with other survivors in the area, including Iron Mike and the Lost Lake camp.
  - Story Impact: This mission marks Deacon's first steps toward forming alliances with other survivors, especially within the Lost Lake camp. It also establishes the tension between factions, as well as the personal toll that living in this post-apocalyptic world has taken on Deacon.

3. "Finding Boozer"

- Mission Overview: One of the central aspects of Deacon's motivation is the well-being of his best friend, Boozer, who has been severely injured. This mission revolves around tracking down Boozer and ensuring his survival after a horrific accident that left him injured and vulnerable to both Freakers and hostile factions.

- o Key Objectives:
    - Search for Boozer in dangerous environments filled with enemies and Freakers.
    - Provide Boozer with medical aid and resources.
    - Protect Boozer from external threats and ensure his safety while you work together to survive.
- o Story Impact: The mission deepens the emotional connection between Deacon and Boozer. Boozer's injuries and his reliance on Deacon underscore the personal stakes of the game, reinforcing the theme of loyalty and the sacrifice Deacon is willing to make for his friends

4. "The Lost Lake" Camp: Joining the Survivors

- Mission Overview: After several early encounters, Deacon finally becomes more involved with the Lost Lake camp and its inhabitants, led by Iron Mike. This mission focuses on Deacon's deeper integration into the survivor community, offering him new opportunities, resources, and story-driven tasks.
    - o Key Objectives:
        - Help Iron Mike and the Lost Lake camp by taking on various tasks such as clearing out enemy factions, gathering supplies, and participating in missions that help stabilize the camp.

- Learn more about the leadership structure of the camp and its role in the fight for survival.
- Strengthen your relationship with key characters like Sarah's former colleagues, who are also fighting for survival.
  - Story Impact: This mission shows the importance of alliances in the game's world. It builds upon the initial themes of survival, but it also expands Deacon's role from a lone survivor to someone who must make decisions affecting the lives of others. His actions here have larger consequences for both his own journey and the story as a whole.

5. "Bounty Hunting" and Settling Old Scores

- Mission Overview: A recurring task in the main story is bounty hunting, where Deacon is tasked with taking down particularly dangerous individuals or groups. This mission involves tracking down bounty targets, which may include both Freakers and hostile humans like Marauders or Rippers.
  - Key Objectives:
    - Hunt down bounty targets across the world of Oregon.
    - Engage in intense combat and stealth missions to eliminate threats.
    - Return bounty items to the camps for rewards, such as money, reputation, and camp credits.
  - Story Impact: These missions help solidify Deacon as a tracker and bounty hunter, reinforcing his role as a mercenary of sorts in the harsh world. These objectives often align with his larger mission of

surviving and finding his wife, but they also provide a moral challenge, as Deacon is forced to make difficult choices about who to trust and who to eliminate.

---

6. "The Ripper Threat"

- Mission Overview: The Rippers are one of the most dangerous and disturbing factions in *Days Gone*. This mission focuses on Deacon's confrontation with them as he tries to eliminate their influence from the world.
    - Key Objectives:
        - Infiltrate Ripper camps and disrupt their operations.
        - Face off against vicious Ripper leaders and their followers.
        - Destroy Ripper symbols and signs of their presence to weaken their morale.
    - Story Impact: The Rippers are not just a physical threat—they represent a terrifying ideology that Deacon must fight against. This mission delves into the dark side of the post-apocalyptic world, highlighting the cruelty of human factions and the destructive nature of their survival tactics. Deacon's conflict with the Rippers introduces moral dilemmas, particularly as he uncovers more about their twisted beliefs.

7. "Sarah's Fate" – The Search for Deacon's Wife

- Mission Overview: One of the most emotionally charged storylines in *Days Gone* revolves around Deacon's search for his wife, Sarah. This mission brings Deacon closer to finding her, revealing new details about what happened to her after the outbreak and how her fate is tied to the larger narrative.

- o Key Objectives:
  - Follow clues left behind by Sarah to uncover her whereabouts.
  - Face difficult emotional moments, as Deacon confronts his past and the loss of his wife.
  - Overcome significant obstacles to rescue Sarah, including hostile factions, Freaker hordes, and the remnants of society's broken infrastructure.
- o Story Impact: This mission serves as the emotional heart of the game. It highlights Deacon's personal journey from loss and despair to hope and redemption. The search for Sarah is more than just a physical journey—it's also a path to healing and closure for Deacon.

---

8. "The Final Confrontation: Endgame Missions"

- Mission Overview: In the final stages of the game, Deacon faces off against the major antagonists in the story and confronts the challenges that have plagued him throughout his journey. This set of missions culminates in a final battle to decide the fate of Oregon and Deacon's future.
  - o Key Objectives:

- Engage in large-scale combat against enemy factions, including the Militia and the Freaker Hordes.
- Make crucial decisions that will impact the fate of key characters and factions.
- Fight for survival as Deacon reaches the climax of his emotional journey.
  - Story Impact: These endgame missions are where all of Deacon's decisions, actions, and relationships come to a head. The conclusion of the game allows players to shape Deacon's ultimate fate and ties up the emotional arcs introduced earlier in the story.

4.2 Flashbacks & Memory Sequences

In *Days Gone*, the story is not told in a linear fashion. Flashbacks and memory sequences provide players with deeper insight into Deacon's past, especially his life before the outbreak, his relationship with his wife, Sarah, and the events that led to the collapse of society. These sequences enrich the narrative by giving context to Deacon's motivations, helping players understand his emotional struggles, and offering hints at the personal losses that continue to haunt him.

1. The Purpose of Flashbacks

- Emotional Depth: Flashbacks in *Days Gone* serve to provide emotional depth to Deacon's character. These sequences often occur during key moments in the game, especially during quiet, reflective moments when Deacon is alone or in the midst of a significant story event.
  - Example: One of the most poignant flashbacks involves a scene from Deacon's life before the

outbreak, where he and Sarah share a quiet moment together. These memories provide players with a glimpse into the bond they shared, making the stakes of Deacon's search for her even more personal.

- Insight into Deacon's Mindset: Flashbacks also reveal Deacon's internal struggles. They show his motivations for surviving in the post-apocalyptic world and his reluctance to form close connections with others, stemming from the loss of his wife. These sequences help players empathize with Deacon and understand why he's reluctant to rely on others.

2. Key Flashback Moments

- Before the Outbreak: Several flashbacks take players to a time before the outbreak, when Deacon and Sarah were still together. These moments provide crucial context for Deacon's journey, showing his life as a motorcycle club member and his emotional connection to Sarah. The contrast between these peaceful flashbacks and the harsh reality of the present adds emotional weight to Deacon's current struggles.
  - Example: A flashback to a moment in their apartment, where Deacon and Sarah are discussing their plans for the future, contrasts starkly with the desolate world Deacon now inhabits. This helps convey the emotional pain he feels at the loss of his wife and the world he once knew.
- The Last Days of Sarah: One of the most significant flashbacks is tied to the final moments Sarah spent before the outbreak spiraled out of control. The flashback shows

the devastating emotional farewell between Deacon and Sarah, offering closure and explaining why Deacon is so determined to find her.

- o Emotional Impact: These sequences are deeply personal, providing players with a sense of closure as they reveal the events that Deacon can't let go of. The emotional significance of these moments is a key factor that motivates Deacon's actions throughout the game.

3. Memory Sequences: An Interactive Narrative Tool

- Exploring Deacon's Past: Memory sequences are an interactive way of exploring Deacon's past. These sequences are not just passive flashbacks but involve player interaction. Deacon often "replays" certain memories in his mind, and players can choose how they approach these moments.
  - o Example: In one memory sequence, Deacon might need to make a decision that reflects his mindset at the time, such as whether to go along with a decision Sarah makes or take a different path. This interaction allows players to explore Deacon's psyche and his internal conflict, enriching the storytelling experience.
- Gameplay Impact: These sequences often offer valuable rewards in the form of upgraded skills, new equipment, or new narrative paths. Completing certain memory sequences also unlocks additional character development for Deacon and other major characters, further fleshing out their backstories.

4. Connecting the Past to the Present

- A Dual Narrative: Flashbacks in *Days Gone* serve to bridge the gap between Deacon's past and present. They help explain why he is the person he is today, highlighting the traumatic events that shaped his survivalist mentality and distrust of others. The juxtaposition between his former life and the present chaos forces players to reflect on how the world has changed—and how Deacon has had to change to survive.
  - Key Insight: For example, Deacon's former role as a biker gang member is shown to be a double-edged sword—while it provided him with camaraderie and purpose, it also led to his disillusionment with the world around him. These flashbacks often show how Deacon wrestles with his identity and how his past continues to influence his actions.

4.3 Side Quests and Optional Stories

While the main story in *Days Gone* is compelling, the optional side quests and stories offer players a chance to further explore the world and its characters. These side activities provide deeper insights into the world of Oregon, give additional context to the main narrative, and reward players with valuable resources, new abilities, and unique encounters. Side quests also allow players to experience the game at their own pace, taking a break from the high-stakes main missions to explore and engage in less urgent tasks

1. Bounty Hunting: Tracking Down Targets

- Overview: Bounty hunting is one of the core side activities in *Days Gone*, where Deacon is tasked with hunting down dangerous individuals for rewards. These bounties range from marauding survivors to notorious gang leaders, and completing them adds variety to the gameplay.

- o Key Objectives:
  - Track down bounty targets and eliminate them, either through stealth or combat.
  - Collect bounty items and bring them to camps for rewards.
- o Story Impact: While bounty hunting is not directly tied to the main narrative, it allows players to interact with other survivors and factions, adding depth to the world. Each bounty is connected to a larger story, giving insight into the state of the world and its remaining inhabitants.

2. Nero Camps: Exploring the Past

- Overview: Nero camps are scattered throughout the world of *Days Gone*, remnants of the government's failed attempt to contain the outbreak. These camps often contain valuable resources, as well as Nero injectors that boost Deacon's health, stamina, and focus.
  - o Key Objectives:
    - Investigate the camps to uncover new lore and find helpful items.
    - Unlock fast travel points and safe zones by clearing Nero camps.
  - o Story Impact: Nero camps provide a unique look at the backstory of the world, giving players a glimpse of the government's efforts to contain the outbreak. These side quests flesh out the lore of the game and connect the past to the present.

3. Encounters with Other Survivors

- Overview: In addition to the main survivor camps, *Days Gone* offers a range of side encounters where Deacon helps out other survivors in need. These missions often provide Deacon with rewards, but they also serve to highlight the moral complexities of the post-apocalyptic world.
  - Key Objectives:
    - Help survivors with tasks like clearing out enemy camps, gathering supplies, or defending against Freakers.
    - Choose whether to help, barter, or engage in more self-serving actions.
  - Story Impact: These side quests shed light on the different kinds of people trying to survive in the world, from the altruistic to the morally ambiguous. They also provide players with the chance to see Deacon's development as he interacts with others and makes choices that impact his character.

4. Freaker Nests & Horde Challenges

- Overview: Freaker nests are one of the most challenging side activities in *Days Gone*, requiring Deacon to clear out nests of Freakers and fight against large hordes. These activities provide an intense break from the main story and allow players to test their combat skills and survival instincts.
  - Key Objectives:
    - Find and destroy Freaker nests hidden around the map.
    - Engage in large-scale battles against Freaker hordes, requiring strategy and the use of powerful weapons.

- Story Impact: These side quests don't directly tie into the main story but help expand on the survival theme. They test Deacon's growth as a survivor, requiring him to take on larger and more dangerous enemies as he progresses through the game.

4.4 Branching Paths & Endings

In *Days Gone Remastered*, the story features important choices that can influence the narrative's progression, leading to different endings. These decisions, whether related to how Deacon interacts with other characters or the choices he makes regarding key events, shape the course of the game. The game's branching paths provide replay value by allowing players to explore different outcomes and see how their actions impact the world around them.

1. The Importance of Player Choices

- Moral Dilemmas: Throughout *Days Gone*, Deacon faces numerous moral dilemmas that force the player to make tough decisions. These decisions, whether related to who lives and who dies, how Deacon interacts with different factions, or his relationship with key characters, all influence the game's narrative. Though many choices are subtle, they often have long-term consequences, leading to different story outcomes.
  - Key Examples:
    - Choosing whether to help certain factions or leave them to fend for themselves.
    - Deciding whether to sacrifice personal goals for the greater good or to pursue revenge.

- The handling of relationships, especially with characters like Boozer, Sarah, and Iron Mike, which affect the course of events.
- Impact on Character Relationships: Deacon's choices have a direct impact on the relationships he has with other characters. Some characters may trust Deacon more or less depending on his actions, while others may offer him assistance or betray him. These interactions not only affect how the game plays out but also add a layer of complexity to the narrative.
  - Example: Helping Iron Mike's camp may strengthen the bond between Deacon and the Lost Lake survivors, opening up opportunities for quests and further storylines. Conversely, betraying or undermining these relationships may limit Deacon's resources and allies.

2. Branching Story Arcs

- The Fate of Sarah: One of the most significant narrative branches in *Days Gone* involves Sarah's fate. Throughout the game, Deacon relentlessly searches for her, with multiple paths potentially opening up based on player choices. The decisions players make will ultimately decide how Deacon's relationship with Sarah is resolved, and whether she remains a key figure in the story or becomes a part of the past.
  - Branching Outcome:
    - If Deacon takes the right steps and uncovers crucial information at the right time, he may be able to reunite with Sarah, leading to a hopeful resolution.
    - Alternatively, neglecting important story events or making decisions that put others

in danger could lead to tragic outcomes where Sarah's fate is left uncertain or sealed.

- The Role of the Rippers & Militia: Two of the game's main antagonistic factions—The Rippers and the Militia—have a significant impact on Deacon's journey. Depending on how the player approaches interactions with these factions, the game's tone can change drastically.
  - Branching Outcome:
    - In some playthroughs, Deacon can actively destroy the Rippers, seeking vengeance for personal losses, and protect camps from Militia encroachment, which affects the final stand-off.
    - Alternatively, failing to deal with these factions or making decisions that weaken Deacon's influence may result in their growing dominance, leading to darker endings.

3. Multiple Endings: A Closer Look

Days Gone Remastered offers multiple endings based on player choices throughout the game. The ending you receive depends heavily on how you choose to resolve key story moments, especially Deacon's interactions with his friends, his wife, and the factions vying for control of Oregon.

- Good Ending: The "good" ending typically involves successfully navigating the conflict between Deacon's emotional attachments (especially to Sarah) and the harsh survivalist world he inhabits. To achieve this ending, Deacon must make the right choices regarding alliances, factions, and personal sacrifices.

- Conditions: Reuniting with Sarah, maintaining strong bonds with allies, and eliminating the biggest threats in the world, such as the Freakers, Rippers, and Militia.
- Bad Ending: A more tragic or "bad" ending occurs when the player makes selfish or short-sighted choices that lead to devastating consequences for both Deacon and the characters he's closest to. In this ending, Deacon may lose key allies or fail in his pursuit of Sarah, resulting in a more somber conclusion.
  - Conditions: Neglecting relationships, making morally questionable choices, or failing to stop major antagonistic forces.
- Alternative Ending: There are also endings where certain characters may live or die based on specific actions taken during the game. These alternative endings can involve Deacon's involvement in larger-scale battles with the Militia, the fate of the camps, or the ultimate fate of Oregon itself.
  - Conditions: These endings are highly dependent on the player's actions and can result in a range of outcomes, from total victory and peace to total collapse, depending on who survives and who doesn't.

4. Post-Credit Sequences & Epilogue

- Post-Credit Scenes: *Days Gone Remastered* also features post-credit scenes that hint at future storylines or provide closure on lingering plot points. These scenes allow players to see the aftermath of their decisions, offering a glimpse of what might come next for Deacon and the world of Oregon.

- Impact of Post-Credit Scenes: These scenes may offer additional context for what happens to other characters, and in some cases, they tease potential new threats that could be explored in possible future expansions or sequels.
- Epilogue: In addition to the post-credit scenes, *Days Gone* provides an epilogue that offers closure for the characters and the world. This epilogue presents a chance for Deacon to reflect on the journey he has taken, and players are given a final look at the state of the world after the events of the main story conclude.

Chapter 5: Combat & Stealth Mechanics

5.1 Melee, Ranged, and Explosives

Combat in *Days Gone Remastered* is gritty, dynamic, and brutal—requiring players to make the most of every weapon type at their disposal. Whether you're going in quietly with a blade or unleashing chaos with grenades, each weapon class has its own strengths, weaknesses, and best-use scenarios.

Melee Weapons

- Basics: Melee combat is crucial, especially early in the game when ammo is scarce. From baseball bats to machetes and spiked clubs, these weapons are silent, deadly, and customizable.
- Durability & Crafting:
  - Melee weapons degrade over time but can be repaired or upgraded.
  - Scrap is your best friend—keep it on hand to keep your favorite bat from breaking mid-Freaker fight.
  - Upgrades can turn simple bats into barbed-wire beaters or axes into devastating tools of destruction.
- Combat Tips:
  - Use melee against isolated enemies to conserve ammo.
  - Perfect for stealth takedowns or tight spaces where firearms are risky.

Ranged Weapons

- Classes:
  - Handguns: Quick, decent in close range.
  - Rifles & Assault Weapons: Mid-to-long range effectiveness, useful against groups or human enemies.
  - Shotguns: Devastating at close range, great for Freaker swarms.
  - Sniper Rifles: Essential for stealth elimination at long distances.
- Customization:
  - Attach suppressors for stealth.
  - Scopes and magazines can improve accuracy and ammo capacity.
- Ammo Management:
  - Always scavenge from enemy corpses and camps.
  - Visit vendors in survivor camps to resupply and upgrade.

Explosives

- Types:
  - Frag Grenades: Great for crowd control or flushing out enemies from cover.
  - Molotovs: Ideal for Freaker nests or lighting up groups of enemies.
  - Pipe Bombs: More powerful than frags—great against heavy targets and vehicles.
  - Proximity Mines: Defensive tools for setting traps.
- Crafting Materials:
  - Most explosives can be crafted using alcohol, kerosene, nails, and other scavenged parts.
  - Invest in crafting skills to carry more or create enhanced versions.

Combat Strategies

- Know Your Enemy: Use melee for lone Freakers, ranged for human encounters, and explosives for hordes.
- Stay Mobile: Don't stand still—use cover, dodge, and reposition constantly.
- Be Efficient: Don't waste a grenade on two enemies—save it for ten.

5.2 Stealth Kills & Tactics

Stealth isn't just an option in *Days Gone*—it's often the smartest way to survive. Especially when you're outnumbered or low on resources, moving quietly and striking from the shadows can mean the difference between life and death.

Stealth Mechanics

- Line of Sight: Stay behind cover and out of enemy vision cones.
- Noise Management:
  - Move slowly through brush to stay silent.
  - Avoid running unless escaping—your footsteps will attract attention.
  - Use distractions like rocks to lure enemies away or create an opening.
- Detection Indicators:
  - Enemies have a white awareness meter—if it fills up, they'll investigate.
  - Red means you've been spotted. Either fight or hide and wait it out.

Silent Weapons

- Melee Stealth Kills:
    o Approach from behind while crouched.
    o Unlock skills to speed up animations and remain undetected after a takedown.
- Crossbows:
    o Silent, deadly, and great for long-range stealth.
    o Recover bolts from enemies or craft them using scrap and cedar saplings.
- Suppressed Firearms:
    o Attach a suppressor to handguns or rifles to kill quietly.
    o Suppressors wear down—replace or repair them regularly.

Tactical Stealth Combat

- Use the Environment:
    o Tall grass is your best friend—hide and watch patrol patterns.
    o Climb rooftops or sneak through windows for tactical positioning.
- Divide and Conquer:
    o Isolate enemies with distractions.
    o Pick them off one by one to avoid group combat.
- Avoiding Hordes:
    o Never engage a horde head-on unless you're fully stocked.
    o Use stealth to sneak past or set traps to thin their numbers from a distance.

Advanced Stealth Tips

- Ambush Camps: Use binoculars to tag enemies and plan your attack route.

- Freakers as Allies: Lure Freakers into enemy camps to cause chaos while you sneak in.
- Night vs. Day:
    - At night, enemies (especially human) are more spread out—good for stealth.
    - During the day, vision is clearer but so are enemy groupings.

5.3 Enemy Types and How to Beat Them

The post-apocalyptic world of *Days Gone Remastered* is filled with threats—both living and undead. Understanding your enemies is half the battle; the other half is knowing exactly how to deal with them. Here's a breakdown of enemy types and how to best take them down.

---

1. Freakers

These infected humans behave like fast, aggressive zombies. They're sensitive to sound and light, and they travel in packs—sometimes massive ones.

- Swarmers: The most common Freakers. Weak individually, dangerous in numbers.
    - Strategy: Use stealth or melee when alone. If they group up, use molotovs or shotguns.
- Newts: Infected children that cling to rooftops and only attack when Deacon is weak or unaware.
    - Strategy: Approach them carefully and take them out with a single melee strike. Don't engage unless provoked.

- Breakers: Huge, brute-like Freakers with high health and devastating melee attacks.
  - Strategy: Keep your distance. Use explosives, focus fire with rifles, and stay mobile.
- Screamers (Remastered exclusive behavior tweaks): Female Freakers that emit loud shrieks to call in reinforcements.
  - Strategy: Eliminate quickly with a suppressed weapon before they alert others.
- Hordes: Groups of 50–500+ Freakers that move as a unit.
  - Strategy: Set traps, use the environment, and keep moving. Take out fuel tanks or use chokepoints to your advantage. Never face them without planning ahead.

2. Human Enemies

- Marauders: Bandits and scavengers looking to rob travelers or destroy camps.
  - Strategy: Use cover, stealth, and headshots. They often have poor armor and can be silently dispatched.
- Rippers: Cult-like enemies who worship Freakers and enjoy chaos.
  - Strategy: Aggressive in combat. Use mid-range rifles or melee if you can isolate them. Avoid being surrounded.
- Anarchists (Remastered addition): Newer faction known for explosives and ambushes.
  - Strategy: Watch out for traps and mines. Spot them with Survival Vision. Take them out from a distance.
- NERO Operatives (Rare encounters): Heavily armored foes guarding advanced tech or research.

- Strategy: Use armor-piercing rounds or explosives. Aim for headshots if helmets are knocked off.

3. Wildlife Threats

- Wolves: Often attack in pairs and are fast.
  - Strategy: Shotguns or pistols are effective. Don't let them flank you.
- Bears: Huge, tanky, and can take a lot of damage.
  - Strategy: Use traps, molotovs, and heavy weapons. Don't try to melee.
- Cougars: Quick and deadly—more dangerous than wolves.
  - Strategy: Use rifles and maintain distance. Stay alert for ambushes.
- Infected Animals (Remastered-exclusive variations): Some animals now show partial infection with erratic, more aggressive behavior.
  - Strategy: Treat like Freakers—explosives and fire are effective.

5.4 Best Weapons for Each Situation

Surviving Days Gone *Remastered* means using the right tool for the job. Here's your loadout cheat sheet for every encounter.

Against Freakers (Small Groups)

- Best Weapons:
  - Melee (Baseball Bat with nails)
  - Suppressed pistol
  - Molotov cocktails
- Tactics:
  - Use stealth kills when possible.

o   Distract with rocks and pick them off silently.

Against Hordes

- Best Weapons:
  - Chicago Chopper (SMG with high damage output)
  - Napalm Molotovs
  - Pipe bombs
  - Remote bombs
- Tactics:
  - Plan your route through narrow terrain or tunnels.
  - Place traps, lure the horde, and use fire/explosives.
  - Don't stay still—run, reload, and strike again.

Against Human Enemies

- Best Weapons:
  - Silenced sniper rifle for ranged kills.
  - MWS Assault Rifle or Stubby Shotgun for CQC.
  - Crossbow with poisoned bolts for silent takedowns.
- Tactics:
  - Stealth kills to thin out groups.
  - Use binoculars to mark targets.
  - Use cover and flank aggressively.

Against Wildlife

- Best Weapons:
  - Shotgun for wolves and cougars.
  - LMG or grenades for bears and infected animals.
- Tactics:
  - Keep distance.
  - Don't get cornered or surrounded.
  - Mount your bike to outrun animals when possible.

All-Purpose Loadout Recommendation

- Primary: MWS Assault Rifle or Chicago Chopper
- Secondary: Silenced Pistol
- Special: Crossbow or Sniper Rifle
- Throwable: Molotovs, Pipe Bombs, Attractor Bombs
- Melee: Upgraded Spiked Bat

Chapter 6: Survival & Resource Management

6.1 Crafting Basics & Advanced Tips

Crafting in *Days Gone Remastered* is essential for survival. Whether you're building a bandage in a firefight or constructing traps for a horde ambush, mastering the crafting system will give you the edge in the wild.

Crafting Basics

- How to Craft: Hold L1 (Weapon Wheel) and select the desired item. Materials must be in your inventory.
- Unlocking Recipes: Many blueprints unlock through story progression or skill tree upgrades.
- Essential Early Items:
    - Bandages: Rags + sterilizer
    - Molotovs: Rag + kerosene + beer bottle
    - Crossbow Bolts: Cedar sapling + scrap

Advanced Crafting Tips

- Fast Crafting: Equip most-used items to hotkeys for mid-combat crafting (e.g., Molotovs or health).
- Ammo Crafting: Later game skills allow crafting ammo for certain weapons like the crossbow.
- Resource Planning:
    - Don't max out your inventory—leave room to scavenge from new locations.
    - Use attractors and traps to set up crowd control before triggering a fight.

6.2 Managing Fuel, Ammo, and Health

In a world without supply chains, you'll need to micromanage your essentials constantly.

Fuel

- Fuel Cans: Found near gas stations, camps, and NERO checkpoints. Can refill your bike or be thrown to explode.
- Fuel Stations: Marked on your map, they fully refill your tank for free.
- Upgrades: Improve tank size to travel longer without refueling.

Ammo

- Scavenging: Loot from enemies, crates, or police vehicles.
- Camp Vendors: Buy ammo when you reach trust level 1 or higher in camps.
- Ammo Reserves: Invest in ammo pouch upgrades to carry more rounds.

Health

- Regeneration: Doesn't happen automatically—use medkits or bandages.
- Crafting: Always have bandages, health cocktails, and adrenaline shots ready.
- Upgrades: Use NERO injectors to increase max health.

6.3 Hunting & Gathering for Supplies

Beyond scavenging ruins, Deacon can also hunt and forage for key survival materials.

Hunting

- Animals: Deer, wolves, bears, and cougars drop meat and crafting resources.
- Tracking: Use Survival Vision to spot tracks and blood trails.
- Traps: Lure animals into traps for safer hunting in dangerous areas.
- Rewards: Animal meat and skins can be sold at camps for credits and trust.

Gathering

- Plants & Herbs: Found in the wild and needed for crafting cocktails.
  - Examples: Lavender (medicinal), Cedar Saplings (bolts), Sterilizer Plants
- Scrap: Found in cars, toolboxes, and buildings. Vital for weapon repair and crafting.
- Resupply Runs: Mark reliable locations (like checkpoints or nests) to revisit for common materials.

6.4 Survival Strategies in Horde Zones

Hordes are no joke. Planning, patience, and panic-prevention are all part of surviving these apex threats.

Preparation

- Scout First: Use binoculars to mark Freakers and note horde paths.
- Set Traps: Place proximity mines, attractor bombs, and fuel barrels in choke points.

- Craft Plenty: Bring maxed out molotovs, grenades, and scrap for bike repairs.

During the Fight

- Stay Mobile: Keep running—never get pinned. Use sprinting stamina wisely.
- Environmental Kills: Lead hordes through bottlenecks, tunnels, or bridges with traps in place.
- Explosives Are King: Pipe bombs, napalm molotovs, and remote bombs thin the herd fast.

Fallback Zones

- Escape Routes: Always plan a backup route in case things go sideways.
- Bike Proximity: Park your bike nearby (facing outward) for a quick getaway.

Post-Fight Tips

- Scavenge the Area: Hordes often guard rich loot zones.
- Regroup: Repair your bike, heal up, and restock ASAP.

Chapter 7: Bike Customization & Maintenance

7.1 How to Upgrade Your Bike

Your bike is your lifeline in *Days Gone Remastered* — it's your ride, your mobile base, and your only way out when things go south. Keeping it upgraded means more speed, better handling, and longer survival.

Where to Upgrade

- Mechanics at Camps: Tucker's Camp (Hot Springs), Copeland's Camp, and Diamond Lake are all equipped with vendors who offer upgrades in exchange for credits and trust levels.
- Trust Levels Matter: Higher trust levels unlock better parts and upgrades.

Upgrade Categories

- Engine: Increases speed and torque.
- Suspension: Better handling off-road.
- Tires: Improve grip and stability.
- Nitro Boost: Adds a speed boost — essential for outrunning hordes.
- Exhaust: Reduces engine noise, making you less likely to attract enemies.
- Fuel Tank: Larger tanks mean fewer stops.
- Saddlebags: Carry extra ammo.
- Visual Upgrades: Change paint, decals, and frames for personalization.

Tips

- Prioritize performance over cosmetics in early-game.
- Saddlebag and fuel tank upgrades are game-changers for long missions.

7.2 Fueling and Repairs On the Go

Being stranded without fuel or riding a half-broken bike into combat? Rookie mistake. Here's how to keep your bike running no matter where you are.

Fueling

- Fuel Cans: Found in gas stations, checkpoints, and garages. Reusable but heavy.
- Gas Pumps: Found across the map and automatically fill your tank when interacted with.
- Fuel Efficiency: Upgrading your engine and fuel tank gives you more range.

Repairs

- Use Scrap: Collected from broken cars, toolboxes, and camps.
- On the Go: Press down on the D-pad near the bike and select "Repair" if you have enough scrap.
- Bike Damage: Hitting enemies or rough terrain can damage your bike. Avoid unnecessary crashes.

Emergency Tip

- Keep 5+ scraps and a fuel can on you at all times before going into horde zones or remote missions.

7.3 Choosing the Best Parts for Combat

Your bike isn't just for travel — it's a tactical asset during ambushes, chases, and escape routes.

Best Upgrades for Combat Situations

- Nitro Boost II or III: Use boost to quickly escape or hit enemies.
- Tough Frame: Increases durability after crashes or taking gunfire.
- Silent Exhaust: Reduces sound, helps in stealthy approaches.
- Saddlebags: Extra ammo is critical during horde takedowns or enemy camp raids.

Recommended Loadout

- Engine: Performance Engine 3+
- Nitro: Boost 2+ (Boost 3 for post-game horde hunting)
- Fuel Tank: As large as possible
- Tires: Off-road tires for better grip during escape

Tips for Combat Use

- Run over lone enemies.
- Circle around camps and take cover behind your bike.
- Use the bike as bait near mines or traps.

7.4 Fast Travel vs Manual Rides: Pros & Cons

Fast travel might save time, but riding manually can lead to better resource management, encounters, and exploration.

Fast Travel

- Pros:
    - Quick movement between discovered camps and checkpoints.
    - Saves real-time for questing and story missions.
- Cons:
    - Consumes fuel and sometimes requires a clear path (no nearby enemies or hordes).
    - Skips out on loot, ambushes, and dynamic encounters.

Manual Riding

- Pros:
    - Experience dynamic weather, enemy ambushes, and random events.
    - Gather resources, encounter survivors, and fight ambushes.
    - Great for earning XP, trust, and loot.
- Cons:
    - Time-consuming.
    - Risky without a fully upgraded or fueled bike.

Best Practice

- Fast travel between cleared camps during daytime.
- Ride manually when exploring, farming materials, or engaging in horde zones.

Chapter 8: Freakers, Hordes & Bosses

8.1 Understanding Freaker Types

Freakers are the heart of *Days Gone Remastered*'s threat ecosystem. Each type behaves differently and requires a unique approach to combat or avoidance.

Common Freaker Types

- Swarmers: Fast, aggressive, and travel in packs.
  - *Tip*: Easy to kill alone, but dangerous in groups—stealth or molotovs work best.
- Newts: Child-like Freakers, usually found on rooftops or high perches.
  - *Tip*: Avoid unless you're injured; then take them out with quick melee strikes.
- Screamers: Females who shriek to summon backup.
  - *Tip*: Prioritize killing them silently before they call more Freakers.
- Breakers: Massive brutes with high health and melee power.
  - *Tip*: Use explosives, keep moving, and hit from range.
- Bleachers *(Remastered variant)*: Stronger Swarmers with pale skin.
  - *Tip*: Aim for headshots or burn them quickly.
- Horde Members: Normal Swarmers, but they act as a single, massive unit.
  - *Tip*: Do not engage without traps, explosives, and an escape plan.

8.2 Horde Behavior and Tactics

Hordes are one of the game's standout features — terrifying, intense, and deeply strategic.

Behavior

- Hordes sleep during the day in caves or dark areas and roam at night.
- Each horde has a path — tracking their habits gives you a tactical advantage.

Tactical Tips

- Plan First: Scout the area. Look for chokepoints and natural barriers.
- Prep Gear: Bring napalm molotovs, pipe bombs, and remote explosives.
- Set Traps: Use attractors to funnel Freakers into kill zones.
- Use Environment: Fuel tanks, tunnels, and bridges make perfect death traps.
- Stay Mobile: Never stay in one spot—run, turn, shoot, and keep moving.
- Fallback Option: Keep your bike parked nearby facing the exit.

Best Time to Fight Hordes

- Night: Easier to lure hordes out, but riskier due to visibility.
- Day: Hordes are resting; perfect for sneak attacks into their den.

8.3 Boss Battles and Strategies

While most of the game's enemies are dynamic, a few high-profile fights test everything you've learned.

Breaker Bosses

- Found guarding story-critical paths or late-game horde zones.
- Strategy: Use cover and dodge frequently. Explosives are your best friend.

Rager Bear (Infected Bear)

- A monstrous infected bear found during story and side missions.
- Strategy: Stay at long range. Use molotovs and hit-and-run tactics. Traps help massively.

Sniper Ambush Leaders

- Human bosses in ambush camps, often with snipers and mines protecting them.
- Strategy: Use Survival Vision to mark enemies, take out snipers first, and push in with stealth.

Remastered-Exclusive Encounters

- Look for "Alpha Freakers" or enhanced boss-like variants with more aggressive AI.
- Strategy: Use terrain and traps; keep adrenaline cocktails handy for healing and boosts.

8.4 Surviving the Night and High-Risk Areas

Nighttime in *Days Gone Remastered* is a whole new game. Enemy numbers swell, visibility drops, and ambushes increase.

Nighttime Tips

- Visibility: Use your flashlight sparingly — it attracts attention.
- Noise Discipline: Use suppressed weapons or stealth kills.
- Avoid Roaming Hordes: Learn their routes or risk running into hundreds of Freakers.
- Better Loot: Risk comes with reward—rare crafting materials often found at night.

High-Risk Zones

- NERO Checkpoints at Night: More guarded by Freakers but yield injectors and loot.
- Infestation Zones: Clear these to make fast travel safer.
- Mountain Passes: Tight terrain means less room to escape ambushes or wildlife.

Survival Loadout

- Weapons: Silenced rifle, molotovs, shotgun.
- Items: Medkits, attractors, flashbangs.
- Bike Prep: Full fuel and max repairs before heading out after dark.

Chapter 9: Camps, Upgrades & Economy

9.1 Earning Trust & Camp Reputation

In *Days Gone Remastered*, each encampment has its own Trust system, ranging from Level 0 to Level 3. Increasing your Trust level unlocks better weapons, bike upgrades, and other resources. Trust is earned independently at each camp, so building relationships across the map is essential.

Ways to Earn Trust:

- Complete Camp-Specific Missions: Engage in bounties, supply runs, and story missions associated with the camp.
- Rescue Survivors: Save individuals in the wild and send them to camps to boost Trust.
- Clear Threats: Eliminate ambush camps, infestation zones, and hordes to earn Trust.
- Turn in Resources: Deliver Freaker ears at the Bounty stand and meat or plants at the Kitchen.

Each of these activities contributes to increasing your Trust level with the respective camp.

9.2 Choosing the Right Camp for Upgrades

Different camps specialize in various upgrades. Selecting the appropriate camp to invest your efforts in can significantly impact your gameplay.

Camp Specializations:

- Copeland's Camp: Focuses on bike performance upgrades.
- Hot Springs (Tucker's Camp): Offers melee and ranged weapon upgrades.
- Lost Lake (Iron Mike's Camp): Provides both bike and weapon upgrades.
- Wizard Island (Crater Lake): Features high-end weapons and gear.

Prioritize camps based on your playstyle and the upgrades you seek.

9.3 Trading, Credits, and Weapon Unlocks

Credits are the currency used within each camp and are not transferable between camps. Earning and spending credits wisely is crucial for acquiring better gear.

Earning Credits:

- Complete Missions: Story and side missions reward you with credits.
- Sell Resources: Turn in Freaker ears, animal meat, and plants.
- Rescue and Escort: Saving survivors and sending them to camps grants credits.

Weapon Unlocks:

Weapons become available for purchase as you increase your Trust level with a camp. For instance, reaching Trust Level 3 at Wizard Island unlocks the powerful "Growler" minigun

9.4 Camp Missions & Unique Rewards

Engaging in camp missions not only advances the story but also provides unique rewards.

Benefits of Camp Missions:

- Experience Points (XP): Gain XP to level up and unlock new skills.
- Trust and Credits: Increase your standing with camps and earn currency.
- Unlockables: Access new weapons, bike upgrades, and crafting recipes.

Chapter 10: Secrets, Easter Eggs & Endgame Content

10.1 Hidden Items and Secret Dialogues

Days Gone is rich with hidden loot and emotional narrative layers that many players miss on their first playthrough.

Hidden Loot

- Fully Crafted Items: Scattered throughout the world are hidden locations containing fully crafted items ready for use. A comprehensive guide detailing these spots can be found on Reddit.

Secret Dialogues

- Sarah's Memorial Stone: Revisiting Sarah's grave after major story events triggers new monologues from Deacon, offering deeper insight into his emotional journey.

10.2 Developer Easter Eggs and References

Bend Studio has embedded numerous nods to its legacy and popular culture within *Days Gone*.

Syphon Filter Universe

- IPCA Stun Gun: Post-game, players can acquire a stun gun reminiscent of the one from *Syphon Filter*, linking the two universesPlayStation

Pop Culture References

- The Last of Us: A house in the game features a scene with a guitar and bloodied bed, reminiscent of *The Last of Us*Days Gone Wiki.

Developer Signatures

- Hidden Signatures: In certain areas, players can find hidden signatures of the developers, serving as a personal touch from the creators

10.3 Endgame Challenges and Replayability

After completing the main storyline, *Days Gone* offers several activities to keep players engaged.

Post-Credit Content

- Secret Ending: Returning to the game world after the credits roll can trigger a secret ending, providing additional narrative closure .PlayStation+1The Gamer+1

New Game Plus (NG+)

- Enhanced Difficulty: Starting NG+ on Survival II difficulty allows players to earn multiple achievements in a single run, offering a fresh challenge .Reddit

10.4 Trophies, Achievements & 100% Completion Tips

Achieving 100% completion in *Days Gone* requires dedication and strategy.

Comprehensive Guides

- Steam Community Guide: A detailed walkthrough is available on the Steam Community, outlining steps to achieve all trophies and achievements . Notable Trophies

- "This Is A Knife": Kill a Breaker, Reacher, or Rager with a knife.
- "Farewell Drift": Accumulate 10 minutes of drifting on your bike.
- "World's End": Complete all NERO Checkpoints and Research Sites .